to

_____

from

_____

Photographs by Pedro Lobo

Roberto de Vicq de Cumptich

love quotes

HarperCollins*Publishers*

HarperCollins books may be purchased for educational, business, or sales promotional use. For information please write: Special Markets Department, HarperCollins Publishers, Inc., 10 East 53rd Street, New York, NY, 10022.

FIRST EDITION

Designed by Roberto de Vicq de Cumptich

LIBRARY OF CONGRESS CATALOGING-IN-PUBLICATION DATA

de Vicq de Cumptich, Roberto, 1958–
    Love quotes / Roberto de Vicq de Cumptich, photos by Pedro Lobo.
    p. cm.
    ISBN 0-06-017419-6
    1. Love — Quotations, maxims, etc. I. Lobo, Pedro. II. Title.
    PN6084.L6L585 1996
    302.3 — dc20
                                                                95-37152

96 97 98 99 00   10 9 8 7 6 5 4 3 2 1

Hearts have as many fashions
as the world has shapes.
—Ovid

to Fearn and Beatriz
from Roberto

to Rita
from Pedro

There
are beautiful flowers that are
scentless,
and beautiful women that are
unlovable.

—*Houllé*

The heart of man has been compared to flowers;
but unlike them, it does not wait for the blowing
of the wind to be scattered abroad. — *Yohida Kenko*

The wrinkles of the heart are more indelible than

—*Dorothé Deluzy*

Love is

—*Japanese proverb*

When distress doesn't show on the face, it lies on th

—*Yiddish proverb*

hose of the brow. *The heart has no wrinkles.*

—*Mme de Sévigné*

beyond reflection.

eart. *All that is in the heart is written in the face.*

—*African proverb*

Love is a

True paradise is not in the heaven

great beautifier.

—Louisa May Alcott

Love built on beauty,

soon as beauty dies

—John Donne

A woman is always a mystery:

one must not be fooled by her face

and her heart's inspirations.

—E. de Amicis

but upon the mouth of a woman in love.

—*Italian proverb*

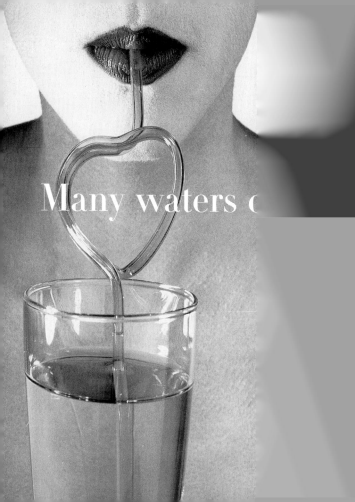

Many waters c

Love and brandy have soothing aftereffects both.

—Mexican proverb

quench love, neither
can floods drown it.

—Song of Solomon

Love, with very young people, is a heartless business. We drink at that age from thirst, or to get drunk; it is only later in life that we occupy ourselves with the individuality of our wine.

—Isak Dinesen

A woman with one lover is an angel,
a woman with two lovers is a monster,
a woman with three lovers is a woman.

—Victor Hugo

One lover, that is love;

two lovers, that is passion;

three lovers, that is commerce.

—French proverb

Love, love, all the rest is nothing.

—*La Fontaine*

Love, love, love

—John Lennon

It is a mistak

to love is

A love defined is a love that is finished.

—*French proverb*

o speak of a bad choice in love, since as soon

as a choice exists, it can only be bad.

—Proust

to choose.

—Joseph Roux

Love nothing

There is only one
kind of love, but
there are thousands
of different copies.

— French proverb

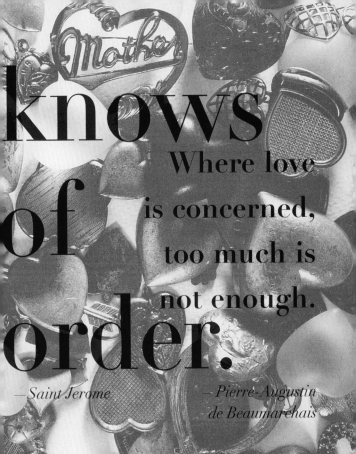

knows

of

order.

—Saint Jerome

Where love
is concerned,
too much is
not enough.

—Pierre-Augustin
de Beaumarchais

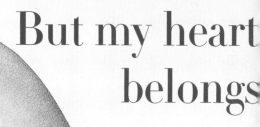

But my heart belongs

One always returns to
one's first love.
— *French proverb*

o Daddy.
— *Cole Porter*

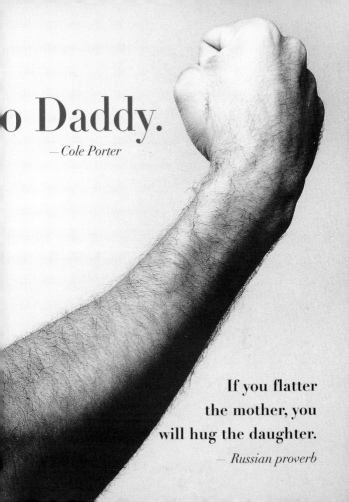

If you flatter
the mother, you
will hug the daughter.
— *Russian proverb*

Love is one thing

lust is another.

— Latin proverb

What they call "heart" is
located far lower than
the four waistcoat buttons.

— Georg Lightberg

Ophelia: 'Tis brief, my lord.
Hamlet: As woman's love.

— Shakespeare

But I will wear my heart upo

When a young man complains that a young lady has no heart, it is a

my sleeve. **For daws to peck at.** —*Shakespeare*

pretty certain sign that she has his.

—*George D. Prentice*

He who is lucky in love
should never play cards.

—*Italian proverb*

He that has luck lead

Love is a game in which
both players cheat.

— *Irish proverb*

—*Dutch proverb*

he bride to church.

Love, love, what slavery is love! —*La Fontaine*

love,

when you hold us in your grasp

loVe,

we can say farewell to caution.

— *French proverb*

Love is many things. But more than anythi

love
feeds only

There is no love sincerer than love of food.

—*George Bernard Shaw*

t is a disturbance of the digestive system.

—Gabriel García Márquez

upon

love.

—Italian proverb

The torch of love is lit in the kitchen.

—*French proverb*

romance is the icing

Love never dies of want, but of indigestion.

—*Ninon de Lenclos*

but love is the cake.

—*Unknown*

To love is human
To be indulgent is

*Little privations
are easily endured when the
heart is better treated than the body.*

—*Rousseau*

also human.

—Latin proverb

To love is to deny oneself.

—Latin proverb

Love and scandal are the bes

In love there is no distinctio

:weeteners of tea.

—*Henry Fielding*

Try thinking of love or something,
Amor vincit insomnia.

—*Christopher Fry*

etween high and low.

—*Japanese proverb*

Love is an exploding cigar we willingly smoke.

—Lynda Barry

Love and smoke cannot be hidden.

—French proverb

Fire in the heart sends smoke into the head.

—German proverb

It requires far more genius t

nake love than to command

armies.
Ninon de Lenclos

Love is like war:
you begin when you like
and leave off when you can.
  —Spanish proverb

Love is a kind of warfare.
  —Ovid

We are easily those we love.

Love makes everything lovely;
hate concentrates itself on the thing hated.

—George McDonald

Thousands are hated,
but none is ever loved without a real cause.

—Johann Kaspar Lavater

duped by

—Molière

ADOLF HITLER
ALIAS
Adolf Schicklegruber,
Adolf Hittler or Hitler

Last heard of in Berlin, Sep... ber 3, 1939. Aged fifty... 5ft. 8½in., dark hair, fr... head. Blue eyes. Sa... plexion, stout build... 11st. 3lb. Sufferi... monomania, with... melancholia. F... into tears when... guttural voice... raising righ... level. DAN...

(Can be recognised full face by habitual scowl. Rarely smiles. Talks rapidly, and when angered screams like a child.)

FOR MURDER Wanted for the murder of over a thousand of his f... countrymen on the night of the Blood Bath, Ju... 1934. Wanted for the murder of countless... opponents in concentration camps. He is indicted for the murder of Jews, Germans, Austrians, Czecho... and Poles. He is now urgently wanted for homicide against ch... British Empire. Hitler is a gunman who shoots to kill. He acts first and talk... No appeals to sentiment can move him. This gangster, surro... hoodlums, is a natural killer. The reward for his apprehens... is the peace of mankind.

FOR KIDNAPPING Wanted for the kid... Schuschnigg, late C... Wanted for the kidna... a heroic martyr who was not afraid to put God befo... attempted kidnapping of Dr. Benes, late Preside... kidnapping tendencies of this established criminal... ...toms before an attempt are threats, black... ...the alternatives of complete surre... ...concentration camps.

What shame forbids me to say,

love demands me to write.

—*Latin proverb*

Love has but one word and it never repeats itself. Love has but one word and it never repeats itself. Love has but one word and it never repeats itself. Love has but one word and it never repeats itself. Love has but one word and it never repeats itself. Love has but one word and it never repeats itself. Love has but one word and it never repeats itself. Love has but one word and it never repeats itself. Love has but one word and it never repeats itself. Love has but one word and it never repeats itself. Love has but one word and it never repeats itself. Love has but one word and it never repeats itself. Love has but one word and it never repeats itself. Love has but one word and it never repeats itself. Love has but one word and it never repeats itself. Love has but one word and it never repeats itself. Love has but one word and it never repeats itself. Love has but one word and it never repeats itself. Love has but one word and it never repeats itself. Love has but one word and it never repeats itself.

—Lacordaire

A thick head can do

a hard

Love is like linen, often changed, the sweeter.
—Phineas Fletcher

s much damage as
heart.
— H. W. Dodds

'Cause she'll never break this heart of stone.
— Jagger/Richards

The head never rules the heart,
but just becomes its partner in crime.

—*Mignon McLaughlin*

Love and murder will out.

—*William Congreve*

What is irritating
about love is that it is
a crime that requires
an accomplice. —*Baudelaire*

Love, like fortune, turns upon a wheel, and is
very much given to rising and falling. — Sir John Vanbrugh

Love
pursues

Economized love is never real lo

There's love in a budg

For a little lo

Love can do much, money can do all. — *German proverb*

Love gives itself; it is not bought.
— *Longfellow*

profit.

— *Irish proverb*

— *Balzac*

Love is the only gold — *Tennyson*

-*English proverb*

Lovers' purses are tied with cobwebs. — *Italian proverb*

ou pay all your life. — *Yiddish proverb*

FOR LOVE IS

BLI

Love is blind, and marriage is a real eye-opener.

— *Unknown*

Love is blinding. That is why lovers like to touch.

— *German proverb*

—*Chaucer*

Who ever loved that love

It was love at first sight. After the wedding
it turned out that he was shortsighted and
she was farsighted. — German proverb

Love looks for love again. — English proverb

A woman with eyes only for one person,
or with eyes always averted from him, creates
exactly the same impression. — La Bruyère

Love at first sight is cured

...not at first sight?
—*Christopher Marlowe*

...by the second look.
—*American proverb*

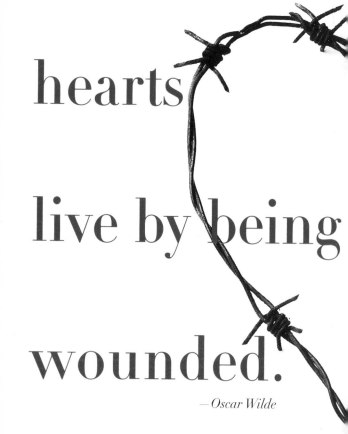

hearts

live by being

wounded.

—*Oscar Wilde*

Where there   is love, there is pain.

　　　　　　　—Spanish proverb

Love is never   without some thorns.

　　　　　　　　—Slovakian proverb

　　　　　　To love is to suffer,

to be loved is to cause suffering.

　　　　　　　　—Comtesse Diane

Love is a disease.

But curable.

— *Rose Macaulay*

Love is a grave

Love is a disease which begins
with fever and ends with pain.

— *American proverb*

mental disease. —*Plato*

*Love is like the measles; all
the worse when it comes late in life.*
— *Douglas Jerrold*

*A lovesick person
looks in vain for a doctor.*
—*West African proverb*

A heart is

love
laughs
lat
locks

You gave me the key to your heart, my lov

ck, but a lock can be opened with a duplicate key.

—Yiddish proverb

miths.

—English proverb

en why did you make me knock?   *—Lord Byron*

We are shaped
by

and fashioned what we love.

—Goethe

Love is not love
Which alters when it alteration finds.

—Shakespeare

Love is a cloth which imagination embroiders.

—Voltaire

Where you sow love, joy grows.

—German proverb

his breast has ever the spurs at his flanks.

Giaccone

Calf love, half love; old love, cold love.

—*Italian proverb*

Love
teaches even
donkeys to
dance.

—French proverb

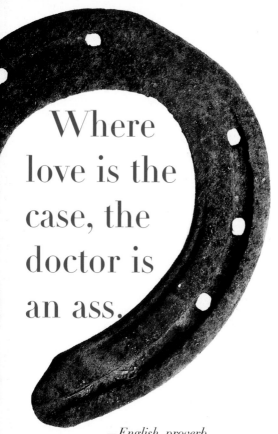

Where love is the case, the doctor is an ass.

—*English proverb*

HO

love is soon

COLD.

—English proverb

too much love

—Philippine proverb

causes

Lovers' quarrels are the renewal of love. — Terence

When love has fallen apart there is no glue

strong enough to hold it together. —Italian proverb

heartbreak.

The human heart
is like Indian rub-
ber: a little swells
it, but a great deal
will not burst it.

—*Anne Brontë*

half so sweet   in

love is   a sweet

No, there's nothing
ife. As love's young dream.
— *Thomas Moore*

*If there's bitterness in the heart, sugar in the
mouth won't make life sweeter.* — *Yiddish proverb*

orment.
— *English proverb*

the heart that

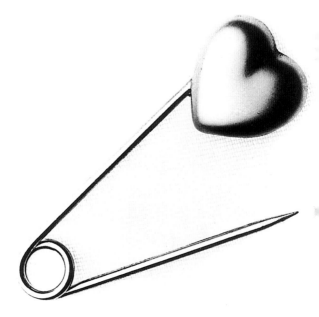

Give a little love

loves is
always young.
—*Greek proverb*

Children begin by loving their parents;
as they grow older they judge them;
sometimes they forgive them.

—*Oscar Wilde*

child, and you get a great deal back. —*John Ruskin*

we should

lov

count time by

love me little, but

love is a sweet dream, and

The richest love
is that which
submits to the
arbitration of time.
—Lawrence Durrell

asses the time, time passes love.

—*French proverb*

neartthrobs.

—*Philip James Bailey*

ove me long.

—*Robert Herrick*

narriage is the alarm clock.

—*Jewish proverb*

You know, a heart

can be broken but

it keeps on beating

just the same.

—*Fannie Flagg*

ACKNOWLEDGMENTS

We wish to thank:

Marc Olivier Alram, Claudia Barcellos,

Carla Brasil, Fearn Cutler,

Ernest Dale, Guilherme Fracornel,

Anna Luisa Marinho, Joseph Montebello,

Monica Rogozinsky, Felipe Taborda,

and Nutmeg.

LOVE IS A GRE

LOVE IS O

LUST IS A

LOVE IS AN EXPLODING CI

LOVE IS A KIN

LOVE IS BEYON

LOVE IS A GAME IN WHI

LOVE IS THE

LOVE IS LIKE LINEN, OFTE

LOVE IS

LOVE IS BLIND, AND MARR

LOVE IS NEVER WIT